Don't

KILL the Sale

Before You Show Up!

5 ELEMENTS Sales Professionals Must Master

to get your head in the game, close more sales,
continually improve and make more money

Using SalesAFFIRMATION!™
(The Pre-Call WarmUp!™ and Post-Call
Critique!™) to generate SalesENERGY!™

By *Therese Samudio*

the Creator of

SuitUp!ShowUp!Sell!™

(A Program of SalesPro Institute LLC)

Dedication

This book is dedicated to you, the sales professional (by design or default), out there every day making it happen. It is true that nothing happens until something is sold and it is the sales performer who makes it happen.

This book is dedicated also to my father (a super star sales pro) who loved sales and helping people and regularly took me on life insurance sales calls with him, and to my mother (a community journalist) who modeled community service and interviewing skills as she took me to work with *her*. They loved people, knew how to work, and were insatiably curious about others' stories.

If you currently classify yourself as a sales professional, this material will really **Up!** your game. And since professionals need to always be learning, there is lots for you here! You will absorb the parts for which you are ready and will want to revisit this material often for review and renewal. Be sure to visit www.SuitUpShowUpSell.com and subscribe for additional information so you will be kept in the SalesPro info loop!

Therese Samudio

TABLE OF CONTENTS

SalesPro Institute LLC

EVERLASTING SALES PERFORMANCE™

Your stories, comments, feedback and
suggestions are always welcome.

Register for FREE resources & updates:

www.SalesProInstitute.com

Preface

"Get out there and sell something!"

The president/CEO/owner of a business usually
started out being the total sales force for the
organization. Often this entrepreneur had no
formal sales training at all but had a pleasant-
enough personality and a product or service that
they understood. Combining that with drive and
the desire to make some money, they did what they
could and personally made some sales.

They knew the business inside and out from the
product and service to the status of the sewer lines
when the toilet got plugged. They started from
nothing, generated some sales and hustled to
provide what had been sold. The emphasis was on
providing quality and service (often at any cost).
After they got busy enough that they had to turn
their attention to running the business (managing
cash flow and producing profit), they decided to
hire someone else to sell.

So, they placed an ad or asked around or in some
other fashion found someone to hire for sales. They
did what they could to educate the new hire on the
product or service and then likely told the rep,

"There's the door. Go find us some customers."

Many sales reps (just like the business owner) have little or no support from above. They must seek out sales education and information on their own. They often don't consciously know how to *not* KILL the sale before they show up. So, they can unintentionally destroy precious sales opportunities before they even get started. The **SalesAFFIRMATION!** process, detailed in this book, will get you ready for each sales conversation so you can close more sales and improve your total sales performance.

Very few people are genuine naturals at this. Some may have natural talent and aptitude, but that will be greatly enhanced with skills and attitude development.

By using *Don't KILL the Sale Before You Show Up! 5 ELEMENTS Sales Professionals Must Master,* you will take your selling performance to a new level!

Remember:

To Earn More: Learn More!

Introduction

I'm Therese Samudio, CEO of SalesPro Institute LLC, and I've had more than 10,000 one-on-one sales interviews with business owners across the U.S. while selling and teaching others to sell management consulting. I've trained hundreds of sales people to close the sale on the first appointment using the information I developed and now have assembled as the program **SuitUp!ShowUp!Sell!**

A journalism graduate from the University of Minnesota, I spent many years in educational and public TV as a writer, producer, director, field reporter and on-air talent. My work aired on public TV in Minnesota and South Dakota as well as in university classrooms and a public school district. I had positions on the staff and faculty at the University of Minnesota and South Dakota State University and also did video projects for the USDA and business clients. I am a sales pro and, at heart, an educator.

What is the purpose of selling? Why did you choose this profession? Well, we all know that nothing happens until something is sold, right? So the noble purpose of selling is to make the world go 'round. But why are you, in particular, in this line of work?

For many people the answer is that they were born this way. They are naturally persuasive and confident. They have always enjoyed being right and leading others to the same conclusion. Others believe in a product or service and become motivated to learn to sell so that they can get the word out about their offering. Sales is not their favorite thing to do, but enthusiasm for the mission carries them along when other natural or learned skills are lacking.

It's important to develop sales skills so that quality performance will consistently be there.

How well you personally invest your time will in large measure determine your level of success.

SuitUp!ShowUp!Sell! includes:

A. *Don't Lose the Sale Before You Suit Up!* **5 STRATEGIES** for **Everlasting SalesPERFORMANCE!** (Work Ethic)

    1) Positive Attitude
    2) Make the Calls
    3) Willingness to Learn

    4) Administration Planning + Tracking = Accountability

    5) Preparation for Calls

B) ***Don't Kill The Sale Before You Show Up!*** **5 ELEMENTS of SalesENERGY!™** (using **SalesAFFIRMATION!**)

    1) The **5 ELEMENTS** are **CONTROL, CONFIDENCE, CONVICTION, CREDIBILITY, & CARING**

    2) **SalesENERGY!**

    3) **Pre-Call WarmUp!** – Part 1 of this book

    4) **Post-Call Critique!** – Part 2 of this book

    5) **The ACTION TRIANGLE**

C) ***Don't Blow The Sale Before You Sell!*** **5 STEPS** of **AffirmativeSELLING!** (The Sales Conversation)

    1) They Buy You

    2) They Buy Their Pain

    3) They Buy Your Process

    4) They Buy Your Company

    5) You Huddle

In ***Don't KILL the Sale Before You Show Up!,*** you will learn to use the **Action Triangle** to develop

5 ELEMENTS Sales Professionals Must Master.

By mastering the **5 ELEMENTS** you will develop **SalesENERGY!** to get your head in the game, close more sales, continually improve and earn more money.

Sales is no longer about stalking prey and pouncing. It is not about tricking people into buying. It's not about taking anything from anybody.

You can plunge in blindly, arbitrarily, trying this and that, shooting from the hip, saying whatever falls out of your mouth and you'll get a certain level of results – and perhaps be wondering why you chose this line of work. Or, you can use the **5 ELEMENTS** to develop your **SalesENERGY!** until it is free-flowing within a disciplined structure.

It is important to suit up and show up and even more important to be mentally prepared for the mission. ***Don't KILL the Sale Before You Show Up!*** gets your mind set, your energy dialed-in for the sales conversation.

Superstars prepare!

They know why they showed up, today. They train and practice and study and use mental rehearsal. Many sales pros talk out loud when alone and hone their best lines. They **SuitUp!** and **ShowUp!** – ready to **Sell!**

PART 1
The 5 ELEMENTS

The 5 ELEMENTS

There are **5 ELEMENTS** you must master so you *Don't KILL the Sale Before You Show Up!* These allow you to get your head in the game, close more sales, perform consistently, continually improve, produce quality sales, and make more money. You will learn to use **SalesAFFIRMATION! (Pre-Call WarmUp!** and **Post-Call Critique!)** to develop the **5 ELEMENTS** that create the necessary and appropriate energy. Your **SalesENERGY!** will make you or break you.

Here are the **5 ELEMENTS** – qualities that I always place in my mind as an attitude adjustment before I call on anyone.

Five Cs. These are the foundation of **SalesENERGY!**

The **Five Cs** are:

CONTROL

CONFIDENCE

CONVICTION

CREDIBILITY &

CARING

I must be in **CONTROL**: of myself, my appearance, my materials, the physical surroundings, the pacing and everything else that happens while I'm with that prospect.

CONFIDENCE: The **SalesAFFIRMATION!** helps you to feel more confident about going into the sales interview.

CONVICTION: If I don't believe in what I'm there to sell, why should anybody else? How can I convey what I don't believe?

CREDIBILITY: What can I do to make myself, my appearance, my company and anything else that I'm doing to present my company, seem as credible as possible?

And the final **C** is **CARING**: When I first started in one sales position I had, I knew virtually nothing about the service that we actually provided. I didn't know why people should want or buy it. But I was totally convinced that we *could* do what we *said* we could and for a year I sold 100% based on my enthusiasm for the service.

I sold more than people who knew a lot about what

The 5 ELEMENTS™

You *Must* Master

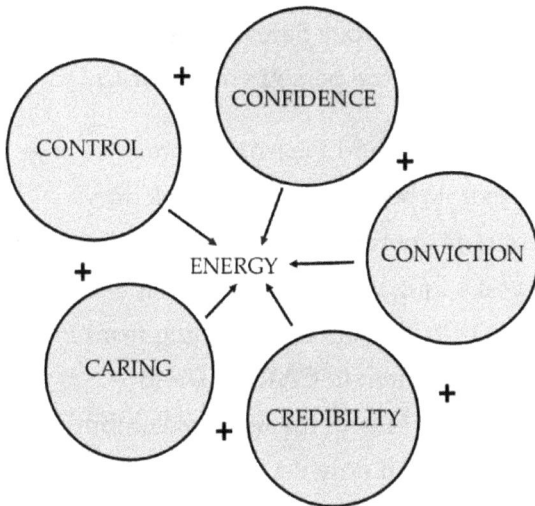

So you **Don't**

KILL the Sale

Before You Show Up!

we were selling just because I believed in it so much. I was excited about it and people would even say to me, "Well, you're sure enthused about this! I guess it must really be good." And they would buy. They were picking up on my energy (in this case enthusiasm/caring). **CARING** influences how you present your **SalesENERGY!** for the offering and for the person you are with.

As time went on and I learned more, I became more credible because of my knowledge. Appropriate energy, even pure enthusiasm, will carry you a long way. My affirmation has evolved with this fifth element transitioning from **ENERGY** as the fifth element to **CARING,** with **SalesENERGY!** being the *result* of combining the **5 ELEMENTS**. Not only do I like the alliteration, but, they really don't care what you know until they know that you care. This is important and it merits a place at the top of the affirmation sequence.

This is where you show that you care about the product or service and how it will perform for *this* prospect and that you care for *this* prospect!

I believe that these **5 ELEMENTS** *combine* to create the ultimate Sales**ENERGY!** that you personify and that will be perceived in a millisecond by the prospective client.

Remember to never pretend to know something you don't know! When I knew little but had enthusiasm it served me well, but there is no substitute as time goes on for actually having some knowledge and wisdom to offer. I was, at any time, only ever a phone call away from talking to someone who had the correct information. Can you arrange to have someone available for you?

CONTROL, CONFIDENCE, CONVICTION, CREDIBILITY and CARING; the **Five Cs that add up to ENERGY** are very helpful for setting your attitude before you go to meet with any prospective client.

CONTROL

+ **CONFIDENCE**

+ **CONVICTION**

+ **CREDIBILITY**

+ **CARING**

_____

= **ENERGY**

PART 2
Pre-Call WarmUp!
AFFIRMATION

Therese Samudio

Pre-Call WarmUp!
AFFIRMATION

"We become what we think about,
most of the time."
– Earl Nightengale

I totally agree with Nightengale's famous remark. He made the point in his classic vinyl recording "The Strangest Secret," recorded over fifty years ago. Nightengale, a pioneer in distance learning, made the recording of himself so more of his sales team could learn from him when he wasn't with them.

In his famous recording, Earl Nightengale credited the concept "We become what we think about" to many great thinkers who had said something similar before he did.

If you accept the premise, "We become what we think about," my question to you is – what do YOU think about before you engage in a sales conversation?

SalesAFFIRMATION! uses a proven and predictable method of mental preparation for the sales conversation and for self-critique afterward.

You will learn:

1) That you are what you decide you are

2) How to write your AFFIRMATION

3) To use the AFFIRMATION as your Pre-Call WarmUp!

4) How to cancel the noise that is in your head

5) How to make a gesture that anchors this strategy

Before a sales conversation, where is your focus?

Are you listening to loud music, talking on the phone, worrying about money, somewhere else mentally? If you are all wound up about your own life and issues, how are you ever going to be available to focus on the prospect's needs?

The sales interview is your game and kick off is imminent. You have to be present. You need to get your head in the game. And you need to do it, right now!

But . . . how?

How can you adjust your thinking to be what it needs to be, right now, on cue? How can you relieve your mind of all distraction so that it can tune in to *this* conversation in *this* moment and be available to serve *this* prospective client?

The answer is to create and use the **SalesAFFIRMATION!** process.

What is the SalesAFFIRMATION!?
SalesAFFIRMATION! is a way to program your mind to help you become more of what you want to be, to get more of what you want out of your selling experience, and to move from sales rep to sales pro. Affirmation means a declaration of truth.

Before you actually use the affirmation that you are about to learn how to write, you will want to make a gesture that brings your attention to this being **ShowUp!** time. One simple technique that I recommend is to cross one index finger over the other and say the word "cancel." That is a signal to cancel out the voices in your head and be present for the affirmation.

When you can't do that, because you are in a place where others can see you, just briefly cross your ankles and say "cancel" to yourself. Or just cross your middle finger over your index finger and say "cancel" to yourself.

Then after reciting the affirmation you can use a fist pump along with a strong puffing exhale or say the word "yes" (with passion). When you can't do that, give a little thumbs up sign.

After a while (when you have developed and used the affirmation consistently and effectively for a long time) you may be able to use these signals as a short cut when you are pressed for time, in place of reciting the entire affirmation sequence. This is *only* recommended when you have extensive successful experience with using the affirmation and have internalized the sequence and is not meant to replace the affirmation every time.

How do I create my AFFIRMATION? You can choose from the affirmation examples given below or create your own. Get yourself to a quiet place to do the writing or selecting.

Affirmation is used before each sales call to get ready, and it's used again after each sales call as your self-critique tool.

What if I don't believe what I'm saying? If you do not believe what you're saying in your Affirmation, then listen to that information. Your lack of belief is demonstrating incongruity. If you still want what you're saying you have or are, then persist and by changing the corresponding habits (using the **ACTION TRIANGLE**) it will become true!

It has been my experience that this process (changing your habits) will largely happen without any special effort on your part. If you decide you don't want it or don't deserve it, you can always lower your expectations and modify your affirmation. But why would you want to do that?

Say that you are just starting to use the affirmation and your sales are not performing. Your mind cannot stand contradiction, and using the affirmation process will make or break what you have going on. Affirmation is very powerful.

Persist and it will bring you into alignment with your stated purpose. Review the ACTION TRIANGLE – you will most likely find yourself changing some habits that are holding you back from feeling authentic.

If you tell yourself that you are prepared, you will change your actions so that you are. The affirmation reminds you what you need to be doing!

You want me to talk to myself? We talk to ourselves all the time. Some sales people feel they have a dialogue going, others feel they have a monologue and some feel that there is a committee in constant conflict holding a meeting in their brain.

What will it do for me? You will find immediately that your subconscious is moving you toward that which you affirm. Each day, your life, your actions and those of the people around you will conform more and more to that which you have included in your affirmation.

Will this process get stale? The affirmation is part of the ever-renewing process of *Don't KILL the Sale Before You Show Up!* The **Sales AFFIRMATION!** is about continual progress rather than static perfection (which doesn't exist).

How does it work? Affirmation programs your subconscious to create in your reality that which you desire. You are in fact what you believe you are. You become what you think about and tell yourself that you are. So be careful what you say to yourself! Tell yourself what you want to believe (do it with emotion and repeatedly) because that is what you will become.

What do most sales people seem to do instead of AFFIRMATION? Most reps do not know this information. They just arrive at an appointment and keep doing the same random things day after day, even though they are often dissatisfied, unhappy, frustrated and wondering why it is not working better. They think their rival has some unfair edge or advantage that they can't ever get.

Remember the old adage that to keep doing what you are doing and hoping for a different outcome is insane.

Reps gripe, whine, grumble, cry and complain about their circumstances. Someone else has a better territory or better comp plan, is kin-of-the-boss or has some other unfair advantage. They blame others for their circumstances. If only . . .

(whatever). But, we only have the power to change ourselves, right?

How will SalesAFFIRMATION! make my sales situation and sales opportunities better? It all begins in your own mind – in your self-talk. What are you telling yourself? Poor me? Poor me? Poor me? People get stuck and stay there. If you keep having the same old conversation in your mind, you will keep getting the same result or worse, since even tactics that were once good do not always produce, forever. We need to keep growing.

If your mental programming is corrupted, you need to re-program your mental software – and *Don't KILL the Sale Before You Show Up!* introduces a simple, no-cost, no-therapy, no-medication, and no-blame way to do it.

Tell yourself different emotionally charged messages about your current reality, and your mind will make your life and performance (and your prospect's response to you) congruent with the message.

I have had one-on-one sales interviews with more than 10,000 business owners all over the U.S. Now, as the creator of **SuitUp!ShowUp!Sell!,** I am sharing with you the sales success strategies and tactics developed from those conversations and the field training I did during those 15+ years.

I am a sales pro. I know, along the way, I have experienced a common sales problem that you've most likely had, too. It is how to **Get Up!** and **Stay Up!** How to stay motivated, how to stay energized day after day, and call after call.

You will learn, here, how to use the Sales AFFIRMATION! and the ACTION TRIANGLE process to get up, stay motivated and always be improving.

Some people perform well for a while and then they fizzle. We call those people a flash in the pan. They were great! They were dynamic! They were exciting! They were breaking all the sales records and then, they died. It all went away. Their performance tanked!

Why? Well, something got them up, something motivated them – for a while. Or, maybe they were just a little short of cash and needed a big paycheck. If you push harder and sell harder and pour on the energy, sure, you can increase your commissions for a paycheck or two. But, you know,

I have staying power. I've been able to achieve high sales, become a high performer and stay that way, day after day, week after week, month after month and year after year. What are people who use the **SalesAFFIRMATION!** process, like me, doing that other people aren't? What's working for them? Well, I have determined that I have to be my own motivation expert, my own best friend. And so do you!

If we use a consistent process we can get a consistent successful result, and make high quality sales (ones that won't cancel) – where you will not find out later that you misled the prospect into a buying decision that was not right for him. Or, where you left out some important information – just plain didn't set the table well. Unfortunately, we've all seen how those sloppy so-called sales can come back to bite us, right?

Did you ever listen to a motivational recording or attend a seminar, and get all excited and go out and do something wonderful, once or twice?

Maybe you performed better for an hour, a day, a week? Of course you have. But then it faded. It wore off. It didn't stay with you day after day after day, did it? And you're going to be selling not just for a few days, but for years and years. How can you get better and better at something? You're studying this material, and that demonstrates that you want to get better at this. Perhaps be constantly improving. Or maybe you want to achieve a higher performance level and sustain that for a long time.

What I have developed and proven over and over works for me, and hundreds of people I've mentored, is the affirmation that I use for the **Pre-Call WarmUp!** *and* the **Post-Call Critique!** (covered in Part 3 of this book). It's something that I've found very, very useful and effective in developing my own performance and *maintaining* a high level of sales performance day after day after day.

Brian Tracy, the legendary sales training guru, once said that early on if he just sat in the car before a sales call and said "I like myself, I like myself, I like myself" and then went in, he sold better. He sold more.

If I said that to *myself* it would not be a good thing. I'd get all inflated with my own importance and not be focused enough on the prospect. But, Tracy got me thinking and wondering if there were other things I could say to myself, and that others could say in this situation, that would program our brains for improved selling success.

I believe that there are, and I know what they are for me. I will tell you what I say before a sales conversation, what I say and do afterward and how this system is designed to improve my (and if you do this, your) sales performance over and over again. If we improve over and over again, we're not just achieving temporary energized performance – but our performance is improving with each and *every* sales call we make. And isn't that what we'd really like to have happen?

What if we could achieve a high performance level and then get better and better and take it to another level? If we continually improve, the possibilities are infinite. The opportunities are endless.

How is it possible to get better with each and every sales call?

The secret is in not letting someone else tell you who you are, and how you should perform, and how to get excited out there, but to tell *yourself* what you need to know and what you need to be. Bubbling over with enthusiasm isn't always the most effective way to sell some services or products. Sometimes you need to be calm and have a quieter demeanor.

Sales motivation recordings, books and seminars don't always teach us how to be calm and controlled. The method you'll learn here will. It will work for you if you need to be excited; it will work for you if you need to be calm. Countless salespeople have told me that when they learned how to use this process, it improved their performance dramatically and they closed more sales!

Here is how it works:

SalesAFFIRMATION! involves constructing a short list of positive and meaningful things you can tell yourself about yourself, your company and your product or service before you sit with a prospect. It conditions your own brain to believe that you can do what you're there to do. And use the **ACTION TRIANGLE** to make the necessary habit changes to develop authenticity.

Then use the exact same list for self-critique following a sales presentation.

You can use this same process to sell on the phone or for video presentations, or for mentoring others, talking with your boss or the sales manager or subordinates, or for sales follow up. The principles are the same. Whenever you need to **SuitUp!** and **ShowUp!** in a sales mode for whatever way you sell, this information will serve you well!

One of the things that I'll put on my AFFIRMATION is:

I am a SalesPro – a great salesperson!

I *am* a **SalesPro.** I believe this about myself. I want my prospect to believe this about me. If I don't believe this about myself, why should anyone buy *anything* from me? I want to tell myself the things that I want my Prospect to believe about me, and I want to believe them myself. If I don't believe them, why should he or why should she? I *am* a *great* salesperson. I'm a Pro. It helps to tell myself that before I go into a sales presentation.

I also tell myself:

I represent a great company!

If I don't believe that one – I should be working for somebody else! I *do* represent a great company. I want to remind myself of that fact before I sit in front of someone else I'm trying to convince about anything. I can tell myself things about my

The ACTION TRIANGLE™

(2) Use the **SalesAFFIRMATION!™**

Before & After

the Sales Call

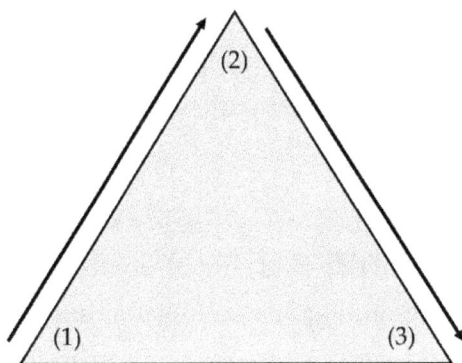

(1) Prepare the
SalesAFFIRMATION!™
(Adapt over time) ⟵

(3) Practice Habits
That Make You
Authentic

© 2003-2014 Therese Samudio

appearance and my desired demeanor. I can talk about my product or service; there are many things I can say.

There are certain things that I need to hear less of over-time and certain things I need to hear more often . . . and, as I find myself exhibiting a certain weakness in my presentation I'll change my **AFFIRMATION** list, my **Pre-Call WarmUp!**, to put something in there reflecting the positive information about that particular concept so I'll improve.

As a matter of fact, every single day before I go into the field, I *do* find something that I want to be working on that day and improving. Yes, every single day, even after years and years in the field and selling a similar service, I find some area that I want to develop and improve in myself. And as a result, I get better every day. You can, too.

Is there something you wish you were better at? Is there something you used to do that you're now forgetting to do? Is there something that other people are doing in your company that makes them better performers than you? Can you learn how to do it? Write it down, make it part of your goal for today. Work on that particular item in every sales presentation and in every encounter with every prospect.

If a day is not long enough for mastery, do it every day for a week. If that is not enough, do it every day for a month. How long will it take for you to become better? Not nearly as long as you think. When you focus your effort you get better very, very quickly.

Right before you walk into an appointment with a prospect, what do you say to yourself? What's going through your head? Are you thinking about problems at home, about overdue car maintenance, unpaid bills? "Do I have to go see this guy again? I've seen him so many times before and all he ever says is 'no.'" Or, "Wow, this place looks really rundown; I'm sure they won't do business with us."

What do you say to yourself right before you walk in to call on a prospect? Do you realize the importance of the thoughts you say to yourself right before you walk in? If you are saying to yourself, "This is not going to be a sale," you seriously reduce the possibility of making the sale. *Don't KILL the Sale Before You Show Up!*

If, on the other hand, you say to yourself that you

are a "**great salesperson,**" that you "**represent a great company**" and that "**this prospect really needs your services**"; if you believe that you "**can help him,**" that he is going to recognize it, and you imagine in your mind him signing that authorization agreement, what are you programmed for?

Then, how will you be feeling when you walk through that door? It's a totally different experience. I've walked in with those kinds of attitudes; I know with which one I can sell better. How about you?

What do you say to yourself right before you walk in the door?

Consider this example: Have you ever said this to yourself (I'll bet you have)? "Oh, I've called on this guy so many times before and he's always told me no." In reality I have (and you may have, too) called on many people, many times, who have always said "no," but that time said "yes." Just because someone has said "no" in the past doesn't mean they don't need what you're offering, today.

Use the SalesAFFIRMATION! process to change your attitude; it _will_ change your results! Each and every time you go in there, go in with the presumption that this Prospect needs what you're selling. Because maybe he or she does. This might be their lucky day. They might be able to do business with *you*, today. Think about it. Doesn't that put you in a better frame of mind? Do you think it would give you better results?

When looking at the AFFIRMATION list that I prepared for myself, I had to ask myself, "What do I want to be like? What do I want to feel like? What do I want to convey? What do I want to have happen in this encounter? How do I want them to feel?"

Just beginning to think about these things puts you head and shoulders above most everybody else who's out there trying to sell.

Most salespeople never bother to prepare at all – they just walk in and say the first thing that falls out of their mouth. They wing it and they *hope,* and sometimes they do make a sale. Well, you can rely on dumb luck and make a sale now and then, and not even know why. But you and I would rather score more often and predictably than that, wouldn't we?

What can I do to look as good as possible? To look as good as is appropriate for the product or service that I'm selling to my prospective clients? What can I do to make my company look and seem as credible as possible? How can I present information in a way that will be believable and well accepted by the prospect?

I don't personally believe in walking in and trying to convince anyone that they should buy anything from me. I don't think I have the right to do that. I think what I need to do is to go in and find out what they need so I can determine if what I have to offer could meet their needs. If it will, then I want to convince them absolutely I have the very best solution to their problem. I want to serve by helping them buy.

If I'm not getting in front of qualified prospects, I need to correct that piece so I can make a legitimate sale to a legitimate buyer.

My job is to find out what their problem is, and then match what I offer with that. Now, I may really believe that everybody I meet really needs what I'm selling (or at least that I want to sell it to everybody). But they have to have some sense that I discovered their need while I'm with them, or they'll feel like I'm trying to force something on them. They may feel that I don't care about them –

like I'm just there to sell them something. The best thing that I can do is determine what their need is and show that I have a match with their need. I want to convince them that what I have will solve their problem, because I believe it *will*.

The **Pre-Call WarmUp!** is about getting your **SalesENERGY!** up; being prepared when you walk in so that once you have their attention, you're going to be able to keep it, you're going to be able to converse in a convincing way and you're going to sell more. I don't know about you, but I always think of myself as self-employed – when I work on a commission basis, that's really what I am. If you work on a commission basis, that's what you are, too.

As a matter of fact, if you sell on any basis other than commission you're still virtually self-employed because if you are not earning what they are paying you, you will not have this opportunity for very long. We are all self-employed, when you think of it that way. We are each like a personal services company that sells our abilities as a sales performer to generate business for the Firm that pays us for our service, right?

OK, I have a prospective client, an appointment set

up with someone that I am going to meet with in a few minutes. How do I prepare myself to go in there to be as effective as possible? What do I say to myself?

And I do mean, say to myself, out loud, with emotion and with conviction. I talk to myself like I mean it, because I do. And, because a lot of times a thought must come out of my mouth, make an audible sound and come back in through my ears in order for my brain to accept it as a thought worth holding onto. Talking to myself out loud, with feeling, with passion and emotion, gets me ready for what comes next.

I print my affirmation list out, laminate it or back it with cardboard and put it in a plastic sleeve – it lives in the passenger seat. In the field, especially, I am never without it.

Imagine I'm sitting in the car parked a block away from the address of the appointment, and I am getting ready to drive over and walk in. I have reviewed my materials; I know for whom I am to ask; I know a little bit about them as much as my advance research will tell me. I plan to verify everything when I am in there. And now, I have to get *myself* ready.

I do the cancel gesture and then recite my **Pre-Call WarmUp!** so I *Don't KILL the Sale Before (I) Show Up!*

And, here is a version of Therese Samudio's

Pre-Call WarmUp!

Remembering to always be in

 CONTROL, to have

 CONFIDENCE,

 CONVICTION,

 CREDIBILITY, &

 CARING, I say those five words out loud with emotion:

CONTROL!

CONFIDENCE!

CONVICTION!

CREDIBILITY!

CARING!

to develop . . .

SalesENERGY!

Then I read out loud the following list:

I am a Sales Pro!

I represent a great company!

I am competent!

I am confident!

I am extremely successful!

I'm having a great day!

I ask appropriate questions!

I listen well!

I get this prospect to talk and interact!

I help this person!

I get them to buy what I'm selling!

I also remember the more he or she talks, the smarter I get.

I ask them; I don't tell them, whenever possible and I *build minor agreements* all along.

Then I do the fist-pump with a loud exhale.

By going through this exercise, I am conditioning myself to go in, be thorough and do a great job. I am conditioning myself to say the right things, and to get the right responses back from the prospect, so I can get them to order my service or my product. I declare the statements in the present tense as though they are happening, right now.

The footnote about the more he or she talks, the smarter I get? It is the more he or she talks *about what I want them to*; the smarter I get. Remember, this is not a social call. We are not just here for a visit. I am a Sales Pro, not a professional visitor.

It is more important to ask a person about information than it is to tell them *anything*. If I know something about them I can say, "Well, I know this about you." But, I would be even smarter if I asked them to tell me something that will give me that same information, even if I already believe that I know it.

The more they talk about what I want them to, the smarter they will think that I am.

People perceive us to be smart if we first talk about things they already believe to be true. It is a fact. And once you get them in that mode, and you introduce new concepts or new ideas, you will be more believable and more credible.

Here's another version of the **Sales AFFIRMATION!** as the **Pre-Call WarmUp!** In a later chapter I'll show you how to use the list as the **After-Call Critique**!

I look great!

I feel great!

I am confident!

Prospects trust me!

I ask great questions!

I'm a great listener!

Prospects tell me their problems!

They sense that I feel their pain!

They believe that I can help them!

They want my help!

I am a great closer!

They buy from me!

What I found is that by reading this list out loud with feeling, with passion, with **CONVICTION** (before I go in) I come out and most of the time, I have to say virtually all of the time, I did every single thing that's on the list. And I close more sales than lots of other people as a result. And my commission checks are bigger than most other people's as a result of this exercise.

Why don't you try it? Write down the list that I have given to you and then modify the list to suit your own situation. As a starter, why not use one of the sequences (whichever fits you better) just as I wrote it?

Try it. Try it for a couple days, and then if you want to make some changes to it, go ahead. Use it before the sales presentation and critique yourself afterward.

The prospect will notice everything about you. He or she will either notice it consciously or notice it unconsciously. I know they notice because often they remark out loud about things – about my appearance, about my car, about my materials, or about my company's credibility or reputation. There are all kinds of things that people will notice.

Have anything they might notice be *noticeable* – presentable!

Be conscious of how you show up from the moment you pull into your parking spot. Often, the boss has his office window facing visitor parking and he's checking you out before you even get out of your vehicle. Be ready; don't be *getting* ready when you get there!

When you make a list like this, it can be a *wish* list, too. You do not have to be living up to everything on this list when you first start out. There may be many things about yourself you want to improve. Maybe there is something about your appearance that is not that great. But, by telling yourself that you look great, you will be surprised at the efforts that you will go through to make what you are saying to yourself be true. You will start looking better because you tell yourself you look great! You will feel more competent and want to become more competent, and go through exercises and lessons and study to become more competent, because you are telling yourself that you are.

Your brain wants congruency between what you are telling yourself you are and what you actually are. Just by telling yourself you're successful you will become more successful. If you can't say with conviction, **I represent a great company**, get a different job. Your honor is at stake. Do something that you believe in!

I ask appropriate questions. If you don't know what the questions are that you need to ask, start asking yourself about the statements that you're saying to the prospect. See if you can turn them around into a question so you can get the prospect answering with the information that you want presented.

Can you help this person? Can you sell to them? If you have used this method once or done it a few times and were successful, analyze what you did right and do it again.

Nothing works with everybody all the time, so you want to have a whole lot of tools you can call into service when you need them. An actor on stage presents the same lines, in the same order, each performance, but the pace and energy change because of the response of the particular unique audience.

For the sales interview, I recommend having a prepared conversation outline that you use every single time that you're with a prospect. But I do not recommend presenting it in the same voice, with the same pacing, to every person you meet. I think it has to be varied. You want to be a bit of a chameleon.

The value of this consistency is that it will become automatic, and you can spend your energy on the heavy lifting, the pain development section of the interview where you find out what the prospect wants. And that is where you use effective questioning to determine which tools you will bring out to use in this conversation.

When I first started selling I thought, well, this is who I am, this is how I am and people can like it or they can leave it. And what happened is some people liked it and some people left it.

I found out I sell a whole lot more when I try to adapt and match and go along with special concerns and needs of the particular person I am with. The more adaptable I am, the more chameleon-like, the more I am able to sell. And that is, after all, why I am there.

I mentioned **Building Minor Agreements**. One example, but certainly not the only one, is a tie-down. A tie-down is when you add something at the end that ties down what you said. "Why, it's a beautiful day out there, isn't it?" That's a tie-down. It's **Building Minor Agreements**. Saying something at the end that asks the prospect to agree with the statement that you just made helps them to make the concept theirs. If you can get the prospect to say something straight out themselves it is even better. More on building minor agreements is also available at www.suitupshowupsell.com.

If you cannot get them to say it straight out, then every time you make a statement of fact you need to determine if you are in agreement on that point. It is essential to verify that you and the prospect are in agreement as you go along. It gets the client or prospective client to buy in to your opinion or to your thought on any subject. And it prevents a surprise at the end when you find out you lost them long ago. Agree all along the way so that the decision to buy is just one more minor agreement. They don't want to disagree with their own opinion. If you bump into a disagreement, resolve it before moving on.

Whenever I do sales training, some of the very most important things I teach involve self-care.

Believe me; you will sell a whole lot better on a full night's sleep than you will on a short one. You'll sell better if you've been fed and properly hydrated than you will if you're hungry and thirsty. If you are tired, hungry and thirsty, it's really tough to go out there and do a good job.

Selling is like performing in a championship athletic competition, over and over and over. It is mentally demanding, physically demanding, emotionally demanding, and spiritually demanding. You have to be exercising all those parts of you so that when game time comes you're ready to compete **MENTALLY, PHYSICALLY, EMOTIONALLY,** and even **SPIRITUALLY**.

How can you be prepared **MENTALLY?** Study, read, watch videos and listen to recordings. These kinds of resources make you a better salesperson as you prepare your mind daily for the task at hand.

PHYSICALLY. Get enough sleep, eat good food. Eat at regular intervals throughout the day. Use the rest room whenever you have the chance (when you need to and when you do not, because sometimes you may find yourself in a situation when you need to and you cannot, and it works against you). Be pro-active on the self-care – be prepared. Drink enough fluids; take water with you in the vehicle. I take water with me in my briefcase. It has saved me more than once. I carry food along, too. The day can get jammed up and I'm not as effective if hungry. Then my energy will be on my hunger and I won't be 100% available to the prospect.

EMOTIONALLY. Pay attention to your own feelings. When you get in there to do a sales presentation, you do not want your own anger or crabbiness or hostility about something that happened outside of that relationship or outside that place of business to affect your ability to communicate effectively with that prospect. When you get into that situation there is only one person whose emotions you should be concerned about, and those are the emotions of the prospect.

So, deal with your own emotions outside and remember that, just like with an actor onstage, when the curtain goes up you have to play your role. As soon as you walk into any prospect's place of business it is curtain up; it is opening night and you had better be ready to perform. This particular opportunity will only come around once. Don't squander it by being unprepared!

Your own emotions need to be set aside unless it's to your advantage to use them. You can arouse your own emotions during the sales encounter if it is to your advantage; just don't inadvertently drag in extraneous ones. Use the **SalesAFFIRMATION!** process to get yourself present in *this* moment for the task at hand.

SPIRITUALLY. This has to do with ethics, honoring your own sensibilities and being true to yourself. If you cannot sell this product or service and be true to yourself, get a different job – it is just too hard and the conflict will tear you up. Do something you believe in.

So, when you put it all together – you feel good, you look good, you think clearly, you are focused on your prospect, you walk in there after having read these affirmations about yourself (out loud, with emotion) – how can you lose?

I believe that as you practice these concepts, as you use the **SalesAFFIRMATION**! as your **Pre-Call WarmUp!** and as your **Post-Call Critique!**, it will change not only the way you behave in the sales presentation, it will change the way that you live and get ready before the sales presentation. You will become better prepared to compete. And remember, you are competing!

You are competing for first the time (and trust) and then the dollars of that prospect. You want that prospect to invest money with you. You want them to be confident enough in you and your performance, and what your company can provide, that they will do business with you instead of with someone else. Play well and win the game. The prospect will be happier, you'll be happier and your commission checks will be a whole lot bigger. Give it a try.

Write your **SalesAFFIRMATION!** – use mine until you have one of your own. Try it! Use it as your **Pre-Call WarmUp!** and when you come out after the sales presentation, use the same list as your **Post-Call Critique**! Remember the **5 ELEMENTS (the 5 Cs that generate your ENERGY).**

This process will help you to get your prospect to open up and share their emotions, to feel something. They will buy on emotion and justify their decision on facts. Other aspects of **AffirmativeSELLING!** go more deeply into those concepts.

Sales, today, is not about sitting someone down and talking them to death until they're so weak all they can do is take that pen in their hand and sign their name because they have no resistance left.

That doesn't work anymore; they have to want

what you're selling. If you do it right, they'll close themselves. "It's time, give me the pen, where do I sign, I want to buy this." Well, they don't *always* literally say that, but when you put the pen in their hand they do put their name on the line. I think it is kind of like the same thing; you have the order.

If you will simply go through this kind of process consistently and practice these **ShowUp! 5 ELEMENTS (**and then, if needed, learn the **5 STRATEGIES** and **5 STEPS** that are the rest of **SuitUp!ShowUp!Sell!**, I believe you will soon be in the top 5% of all the sales producers in this country because you'll be walking in better prepared than, I estimate, 95% of the rest of the reps out there.

Which group do you want to be in, the top 5% or the vast majority of people who go out every day unprepared and just see what happens? Of course you'd rather be a top performer! Who wouldn't?

It takes the same amount of time to do this well as to underperform. We each get 24/7 every week. How are you choosing to invest your time? Use your time well. Work smart. Give it a try. I know you'll be pleased.

And, consider this:

Set your mind on helping and you will feel calmer.

Set your mind on listening and you will be more interested.

Set your mind on serving and you will sell well – what they need that will get them what they want, and you will always be able to go back to that client (to that well) for more business (and to turn them into your champion).

Set your mind on being positive – you will sell well and in a cooperative and non-adversarial way.

Set your mind on honesty and you will *be* authentic and you will sell well.

Set your mind on kindness and you will sleep well while you sell well – your prospect is a person, not prey.

Set your mind on gratitude and you will sell well – and appreciate each new learning experience.

Set your mind on greatness and you will sell well – and you will believe what you repeat.

Set your mind on ethical performance and you will sell well – you will only represent a product and company you believe in.

Set your mind on your goal and you will sell well – you will get farther every time.

Remember, you can call on unseen forces to come to your aid, too (a la Napoleon Hill in his classic book *Think and Grow Rich*).

If you reach for the stars and land on the moon, you will have gone farther than if you had not set a goal.

Money, like love, cannot (legitimately) be sought directly. It is a byproduct of how you choose to live and serve. If you need more of either, look inside and examine how you live and serve.

Selling well is not taking something from someone, but bringing benefit to someone in exchange for a consideration of similar value.

To sell well is to understand the difference between features and benefits. Features are about you. Benefits are about them. And you need to know the prospect a bit in order to determine if any of those benefits are relevant to the needs of this person. The sale is about them, not you!

Control in a sales encounter is about controlling the situation and the conversation. In order to control the prospect (guide the progress of the conversation) you must first master self-control. *You* are the one in need of control.

For fearlessness and unshakeable self-confidence: Verify you have all that you need prepared in advance. I always take the same number of pens, pencils and back-up materials, contracts, etc. I do this so I won't have to think about it during the call, knowing I'm totally prepared. I want all my energy available for the prospect/client.

Combine material preparedness with the **SalesAFFIRMATION!** process and you just may become unstoppable!

REVIEW

Select one of the **SalesAFFIRMATION!** sequences above.

Write it in Part 4 of this book as **Your Affirmation #1**.

Remind yourself of the facet of your performance you are working to improve today.

Note it at the bottom of your Affirmation.

Have this book with you as you make your calls.

Use your affirmation as your **Pre-Call WarmUp!** (prior to *every* sales conversation).

Part 3
Post-Call Critique!
AFFIRMATION

Post-Call Critique!
AFFIRMATION
"We become what we contemplate."
– Plato

Did you hear the one about the lavish dinners that my mother used to serve? The centerpiece was the roast; it was perfectly browned, juicy and absolutely delicious! This was back in the day when she'd fix Sunday afternoon dinner for the extended family. The day included picking up a relative from the "old folks" home and having him over for home cooking and company.

She would serve the beef roast on a big platter and I noticed every time that the ends of the piece of meat had been removed before she roasted it. I was setting up a household of my own at the time and collecting recipes. I asked her about how she prepared this dish, one of my all-time favorites.

As she began the instructions, she told me about how she selected the roast and that before she put it in the oven she'd cut off both ends.

I stopped her at this point in the story and asked her why she did that. With the meat being sold by the pound why would you do that?

She explained that she'd actually gotten the recipe from *her* mother and that was what Grandma had always done. She did not know why. So the next time I made a trip to Grandma's house, I decided to ask her about this.

As luck would have it she was serving roast beef! And I inquired about her technique. Grandma explained that her roasting pan was too small for the whole thing – that was why she always cut the ends off. My mother had just imitated *her* mother.

Is there something in your sales process that you are doing in imitation of someone else? Are you even aware that you might be doing this? Do you have any idea why they did it that way? Have you looked at your sales process and preparation to see if it could be better?

Could some other tactic be more efficient and give you a better result?

Do you review your metrics and look for ways to improve? The SalesAFFIRMATION! process uses a proven and predictable method of mental preparation for the sales conversation and for self-critique afterward.

You will:

1) Evaluate your performance – every time
2) Re-use the **SalesAFFIRMATION!** as your critique tool
3) Be fearless in your review

Re-use the SalesAFFIRMATION! – pluses first, then what you will do or be differently next call.

1) Re-read your affirmation sequence.
2) What did you do right?
3) Were you prepared physically and mentally?
4) How can you perform better next time?
5) Did you make the sale?
6) Find ways to celebrate your success – to reward yourself and those who support you.
7) Share your success to inspire others!

Here is a version of Therese Samudio's

Post-Call Critique!:

I look great!

I feel great!

I am confident!

Prospects trust me!

I ask great questions!

I'm a great listener!

Prospects tell me their problems!

They sense that I feel their pain!

They believe that I can help them!

They want my help!

I am a great closer!

They buy from me!

Ask yourself, "Did I display all of the qualities that I had on my **AFFIRMATION**, my **Warm-Up!** list? Did I exhibit all the listed positive traits? Did I present my company so that it would reflect the positive traits that I have on my list?"

A very important strategy for self-critique following a sales presentation is to always, always,

always begin with the positive. The very first thing to do after any sales presentation is to review what you did right before ever noting anything that needs to be done differently in the future. And that is what criticism should be viewed as, not "Oh no, look what I did wrong. I really blew that." Rather, make it about what you can do better next time.

Suppose you had an appointment, and you believe things went well. What is your definition of "well"? Did you make the sale? That is the best way things can go, right? Did you progress the sale? But, you know every appointment can teach you something – even the ones where you do not sell. Whether you sold or did not make the sale, after the appointment ask yourself, did I do what was on my **Pre-Call WarmUp!**?

Did you remember the 5 ELEMENTS, the "5 C's"? Ask yourself, did you stay in **CONTROL**? And I have somewhat of a reputation (some people I work with have called me the Interior Decorator) because I like to move prospects' furniture around. I do not like to sit where they tell me to sit; I like to tell them where to sit. I do not like to put my materials where they want them; I like to put them where I want them. I like to take control of the whole encounter with the prospect, while at the same time letting him feel like he or she is in control. So *were* you in **CONTROL**?

Did you seem **CONFIDENT**? Did you have **CONVICTION**? Did you seem **CREDIBLE**? Were you **CARING?** Did you come in with the right **ENERGY** (The combination of the **5 ELEMENTS**)? If you can answer yes to this, then boy, that *was* a satisfying experience, wasn't it?

In the Post-Call Critique!, remember to be positive before you say anything negative to yourself.

Give yourself strokes for everything that went right. For example: the prospect was there (extra points if he was expecting you). If you got him to sit down when he was telling you he really could not, that is worth points. Sometimes they will say, "I know you were supposed to be here but I can't see you now," and you are still able to get them to sit down for an hour and half. Perhaps you had told them that you just "need two minutes" and by the time you got into the two minutes they were so interested they did not ask you to leave!

So, give yourself points if you actually got them to sit. Get points if you got them to tell you their problems. And, of course, you get points if you were able to close the sale. Give yourself points.

Rate yourself on your performance.

Could they tell you like yourself? Could the prospect tell you are competent, did that show? You are **CONFIDENT**, did that show? You are extremely successful. How can you show that? Did you show that by your voice, by your demeanor, by how you appeared, by your materials being clean, neat and orderly? By being organized, not random? By looking good?

I am a SalesPro – a great salesperson! Could they tell that? Could they know, could they tell, did they feel they were dealing with a winner? **I represent a great company!** Did you present your company well enough that they would feel that way about it? **I am having a great day!** Or did you go in there downtrodden, shoulders hunched over, looking like it was Friday at four o'clock and you were all wrung out?

Did you ask questions? Or did you just sit there and blather on and on about yourself or other extraneous matters? Did you listen? **I listen well!** That's on the list. Did you listen? Did you hear what they were saying? Did you respond? Did you ask appropriate questions? Did you listen and then take what they were saying and move the dialogue back where you wanted the prospect to be?

Did you get the prospect to talk and interact – not just about anything, but about what you wanted them to talk and interact concerning? **I can help this person!** Could they tell that? Did they believe that? **I can get them to buy what I'm selling.** Did they buy? Did they order right now? Did they schedule a callback? Where *are* you in the sale? Did you make the progress that you wanted?

Can you see how self-critique after a sales call will help you to do better next time?

If you use the affirmation sequence where I said **I look great! I feel great! I'm confident! Prospects trust me! I ask great questions! I'm a great listener! Prospects tell me their problems! They sense that I feel their pain! They believe I can help them! They want my help! I'm a great closer! They buy from me!;** review that line by line by line. Did you do what you set out to do?

Try it! You can review this material over and over again. You can also obtain an audio version of this material at www.suitupshowupsell.com.

There are all kinds of things you can do to be in a better position to sell, aren't there? I had my briefcase with me. I had two pens with me. I had my calendar and the appropriate electronic devices. I was ready to make notes. Everything looked neat and clean and was orderly. My hair was styled. My clothing was carefully selected. Everything was shipshape when I walked in there. My car was clean; you'd be amazed by how many times they've followed me out to my car or commented, "Well, you have a nice car; I like your car; what kind of a car is that?"

Remember, start with the positive; tell yourself what you did right. Give yourself credit for everything. I got up on time. I was dressed and ready to go. I had a decent breakfast. I took water with me. I remembered to use the rest room before I went in. Everything!

Doing a critique after each and EVERY sales conversation will, in my experience, dramatically improve your performance.

REVIEW

Use your **Pre-Call WarmUp!** as your **Post-Call Critique!** after *every* sales call.

Ask yourself, "Did I do everything that was on my list?"

Referring to the note at the bottom, ask yourself if you *are* working to improve in that area today.

Keep *that* note on your **SalesAFFIRMATION!** until you have mastered it.

When you have mastered that one, choose another.

After a while, modify one line or two of the Sales**AFFIRMATION!** so it will better suit your current needs.

Periodically decide if you need a more dramatic re-write of your **SalesAFFIRMATION!**

Use versions 2, 3, and 4 in Part 4 of this book to write the modified SalesAFFIRMATION!

Remembering the **ACTION TRIANGLE**, review (daily) your habits and see if you are behaving in a way that makes you feel authentic.

Part 4
Your AFFIRMATION

Part 4   **YOUR AFFIRMATION #1**

What area of improvement are you focusing on, today? _____

Date _____

CONTROL

CONFIDENCE

CONVICTION

CREDIBILITY

CARING

ENERGY

_____

_____

_____

_____

_____

_____

_____

_____

_____

NOTE: _____

Part 4   YOUR AFFIRMATION #2

What area of improvement are you focusing on, today? _____

Date _____

CONTROL

CONFIDENCE

CREDIBILITY

CONVICTION

CARING

ENERGY

_____

_____

_____

_____

_____

_____

_____

_____

_____

NOTE: _____

Part 4   **YOUR AFFIRMATION #3**

What area of improvement are you focusing on, today? _____

Date _____

CONTROL

CONFIDENCE

CONVICTION

CREDIBILITY

CARING

ENERGY

_____

_____

_____

_____

_____

_____

_____

_____

NOTE: _____

Part 4   **YOUR AFFIRMATION #4**

What area of improvement are you focusing on, today? _____

Date _____

CONTROL

CONFIDENCE

CONVICTION

CREDIBILITY

CARING

ENERGY

_____

_____

_____

_____

_____

_____

_____

_____

_____

NOTE: _____

SalesAFFIRMATION! is available
in audio format for MP3 download
or as a CD

http://affirmativeselling.com/recommended-tools/

Email: info@affirmativeselling.com

Part 5
Additional Resources

Additional Resources

7 Steps for
Effective Sales
Communication
When Your Normal
Flow is Interrupted

So You Will Keep Your
Foot Out of Your Mouth
& Close More Sales

FREE eBook

Therese Samudio

Register at www.SuitUpShowUpSell.com for Therese's FREE ebook: *7 Steps for Effective Sales Communication When Your Normal Flow is Interrupted* So You Will Keep Your Foot Out of Your Mouth & Close More Sales

Opt In for FREE sales training resources at
www.SalesProInstitute.com

Review FREE VIDEOS and written blog articles on
sales strategies and tactics at
www.SuitUpShowUpSell.com (Blog)

Audio version of **SalesAFFIRMATION!** concept
available at www.AffirmativeSelling.com (Shop)

Purchase the audio "**SalesGATEKEEPERS!™** How
to Befriend the Screener in 10 Seconds or Less!
Available at
www.AffirmativeSelling.com (Shop)

For quantity pricing: Contact the publisher

☆☆☆☆☆

Information on appearances by Therese Samudio:
keynotes, breakout sessions, seminars, workshops,
peer groups, and mentor progam is available at
www.ThereseSamudio.com

Like/Follow us on . . .

Facebook: Therese Samudio – Affirmative Selling

Twitter: @ThereseSamudio

LinkedIn: www.linkedin.com/in/theresesamudio/

Affirmative
SELLING!™

A Program of SalesPro Institute LLC

Your comments, success stories, feedback and suggestions are always welcome.

FREE subscription for ongoing sales education and resources is available at:
www.SuitUpShowUpSell.com

Contact: info@AffirmativeSelling.com

Please keep in touch. Thank you.

SNEAK PEEK

SalesGATEKEEPERS!
How to Befriend the Screener
in 10 Seconds or Less!

**Following is a Preview the transcript
for the first several minutes of this
Sales Audio Program**

MP3 and CD available from

http://affirmativeselling.com/recommended-tools/

SalesGATEKEEPERS!
How to Befriend the Screener in 10 Seconds or Less!

"Hi, I'm Therese Samudio from XYZ Company, may I please speak to Mike?" Now, that didn't sound too bad, did it? But let me tell you, if you study the rest of this material and apply the principles that I'm about to teach you, you'll begin to think that is one of the worst telephone openings you've ever heard.

Even at the front desk of the business you're calling on, just announcing who you are there to visit is a very common and not-so-hot practice. The information on this recording will help you work well with the person who stands between you and your prospect – that VIP, the gatekeeper.

I'm Therese Samudio, CEO of SalesPro Institute LLC, and I want to thank you for ordering this material. I promise, I won't waste your time and you'll learn valuable principles and concepts, today, that have been identified to increase your sit percentage, your closing rate, your value to your

Company and, most importantly, your income.

I've had one-on-one sales interviews with more than 10,000 business owners all over the U.S. and trained and coached hundreds of outside sales reps to improve their own sales performance. The material presented here was developed from that experience.

This was new information to all but the tiniest minority of sales reps I have ever worked with. The few who were already doing something like this always outperformed their peers. Since you want to outperform your peers and certainly want to perform better today than you did yesterday, you will benefit from this information.

If you ever want to have a meeting with a prospective client, you have to get through a gatekeeper. Is a gatekeeper only a receptionist? No. A gatekeeper is any person who stands between you and your prospect, the decision maker. It may be someone on the telephone; it may be someone who answers a door or sits at the reception desk.

It may be someone who screens electronic communications. It may be a person who stands physically between you and yet another gatekeeper.

I think of a gatekeeper as the very first person I see or speak with when attempting to contact a prospective client. As a matter of fact, I think of a gatekeeper *as* a prospective client because if I can't get through them, I can't get anywhere.

So my first sale is always the gatekeeper. Yours is, too.

Dale Carnegie told us that the sweetest sound any person can ever hear is what? That's right. The sound of their own name. Do you know the name of your gatekeeper? How can you find it out? Is it important to know the gatekeeper's name? I believe it's absolutely critical to know the gatekeeper's name and to use it as often as possible.

Each and every time you have contact with the gatekeeper – any person who stands first, second or third between you and your prospect – know their name. And how can you know the person's name? Do you have to do elaborate research? Have military intelligence working for you? Go online and Google them or do a background check? Not necessarily.

Often, the best way is also the simplest way. Just introduce yourself and ask what their name is – and then use it! "Hi, I'm Therese Samudio, who are you?" "Hi, I'm Therese Samudio, and I'm so glad to meet you." Then pause. They will always reply, "Well, hi, I'm Tina" (or Barbara or Fred). People want to tell you their name and then you reply, "Hi, Tina, it's so nice to meet you" and pause.

Now, what does this have to do with me getting through to see the person that I want to see? Everything! It has everything to do with me getting through to see the person that I want to see. And if I can't see someone, I can't sell them. I have to get through to the person that I want to see.

Let's look at this from a telemarketing point of view for a moment. You may have a telemarketer, a business coordinator, an appointment setter who works specifically for you. Or, you may *be* your own appointment setter. The principles and concepts that I'm presenting here apply to both situations. Let's look at it from the perspective that you're calling and setting appointments for yourself. This is the technique that I recommend you use on the telephone.

"Hi, I'm Therese Samudio from XYZ, to whom am I speaking, please?" The person who answered the telephone will be so surprised that you asked for them by their name and treated them like a person that they'll probably pause for a second before they reply. Then, they may say something like, "Well, I'm Bonnie." "Well, hi, Bonnie," you reply, "It's so nice to meet you." Or "It's so nice to speak with you" or "Oh, yes, Bonnie." Any one of these will work. And each one presents a different level of familiarity which may be appropriate for the kind of company that you're calling on . . .

(This is just the beginning!)

SalesGATEKEEPERS! is available
in audio format for MP3 download
or as a CD

http://affirmativeselling.com/recommended-tools/

Email: info@affirmativeselling.com

About SuitUp!ShowUp!Sell!

You can be more, do more and earn more by helping more people get what they want. Learn to sell and sell well and all your own dreams will come true. Sales is all about helping others. And everybody sells! Is sales in your job title? Then you sell. Is sales not in your job title? You still sell. The skills and habits needed can be learned and you can be a sales superstar.

Own a business? That's a huge sales job. You sell all the time. Need to find a new client or get a repeat order? How about getting hired to provide services, recruiting a new employee, or lining up a loan? All sales!

Does your job title say Sales? Hey, this is your bread and butter. Want to "Up" your game?

Looking for a job? That's a big targeted sales job. Learn to sell well and you will create not just this job but ever-renewing habits for job security.

Nothing happens until something is sold. It's true!

Epilogue

The best preparation leads to the best results.

Continual improvement is the name of the game. If you want to be a Superstar SalesPro, you need to recognize this is like a championship sports competition with a twist. When you practice the discipline of **SuitUp!ShowUp!Sell!** you both win. Both you and the client win. Neither loses.

You **SuitUp!** (to get in front of enough qualified prospects) by using the **5 STRATEGIES** for **Everlasting SalesPERFORMANCE!** Then, you get ready to **ShowUp!** (using **SalesAFFIRMATION!**). And then you **Sell!** (by determining what a particular prospect wants through the **AffirmativeSELLING!** conversation). By coming to agreement on how your offering will provide them with what they need that will get them what they want, they become your client.

Don't KILL the Sale Before You Show Up! is a resource for the sales pro (who is hired to bring in business – often with no guidance from above), the sales manager and the business CEO, who is often also the chief revenue officer (CRO) and who is personally selling. It speaks to those who need quality sales, more consistently. It will help you sell better and help you support the sales effort if you are in a position of leadership.

Don't KILL the Sale Before You Show Up! can help you both close more sales and improve your total team's performance.

To Earn More: Learn More!

The Author

Therese Samudio, founder and CEO of SalesPro Institute LLC, is a sales expert who thoroughly enjoys delving into and resolving sales challenges with teams, team leaders, and individuals. She has accumulated a wealth of sales knowledge while interviewing over 10,000 business owners all over America while selling and teaching others to sell management consulting services as CEO, president, vice president, sales performer, sales mentor, peer group director, and sales coach/trainer for her own businesses, two national management consulting firms and a regional peer group organization.

A professional public speaker, workshop and sales program presenter, author, sales coach, educator and blogger, she is recognized nationally for producing **Quality** sales **Consistently**.

She is the creator of **Suit Up!Show Up!Sell!** (**5 STRATEGIES** for **Everlasting Sales PERFORMANCE!, 5 ELEMENTS** of **SalesENERGY!** – including the **SalesAFFIRMATION!** process and the **ACTION TRIANGLE,** and **5 STEPS** of the **AffirmativeSELLING!** conversation**).** She has a great respect and fondness for **GATEKEEPERS** (screeners) and also educates on that topic.

Her background also includes providing advertising, PR and special events services for 500 retail businesses in 15 shopping malls in the Midwest. "My frustration with sales promotion is that top line sales are only part of the picture – important, critical, but not a guarantee of profit or longevity. You have to know how to manage and control the entire business in order to prevail. And you must manage your life as well. I really enjoy helping business professionals in sales, total business and life improvement."

A journalism graduate from the University of Minnesota, she spent many years in educational and public TV as a writer, producer, director, field reporter and on-air talent. Therese's work aired on public TV in Minnesota and South Dakota as well as in university classrooms and a public school district. She was on the staff and faculty at the University of Minnesota and South Dakota State University and also did video projects for the USDA and business clients. She is a sales pro and, at heart, an educator.

Acknowledgements

I have many people to thank for their support during the creation of this book. ***Don't KILL the Sale Before You Show Up!*** took more than ten years from concept to clarification to publication with research going back another ten; to try to name all those who had input would be impossible.

I do wish to specifically thank all the more than 10,000 business owners I have had the honor of interviewing (that was my research laboratory), the businesses that have signed my paycheck and provided continual sales education, and the many fine colleagues with whom I have worked and studied. Many of them have become lifetime friends. I also appreciate the scores of sales reps I have mentored. I learned something from each one of the above.

In the most recent years I have enjoyed excellent technical expertise and continual moral support from Steve Lenius, my editor and designer. I am also grateful to Mary Emfield, my friend of many years, for her technical help, unwavering support, and continual encouragement.

Therese Samudio

Testimonials

"(The Business Owners in your AffirmativeSELLING! Workshop said) they would use what they learned to improve their sales. (They want) more from Therese. (To quote one), 'I learned important nuggets of information to help my business.' I highly recommend Therese and her Sales Affirmation Workshop. She is an energetic and engaging speaker that has mastered the art of sales!" Sarah Patnode, Director of Professional and Organizational Development, Professional & Workforce Training, Anoka Technical College and Anoka Ramsey Community College

"I believe that (SuitUp!ShowUp!Sell!) is a new and viable methodology . . . quite effective in today's selling atmosphere. I say this because (the) underlying message addresses new and needed changes to practices that have become obsolete and other concepts that have been totally overlooked by others." Thom Marin (Business Owner), DataTech Solutions LLC

"It's been said that 'those who can, do and those who can't, teach.' When it comes to selling, Therese Samudio does BOTH with passion and ease. She can really deliver a keynote, inspire and move people to action. In the field, she's a fearless closer. I've followed her brilliant work for years. As a sales coach or mentor (she has influenced me along the way) – the best! When she works with you or your organization, you'll be in most capable hands." Dianne Rentschler, National Sales Manager, HIG, Inc.

(About her SuitUp!ShowUp!Sell!™ appearance for Edina Business Professionals) "Therese gave me some new ideas when speaking to prospects. Realized some mistakes I might be making. Good energy." Joe Rapacki, CPA, Rapacki & Company.

(About her workshop) "(I appreciated Therese's) direct/compact (style) and her extensive field (selling and training) experience, variety of industries and track record." David Anderson, Attorney, Mahoney Anderson LLC

"Just want to let you know that I do practice repeating the nine statements that you asked me to put down about cold-calling. It worked! I am no longer dreading the phone or the stranger in front of me when I speak with them about my speaking services or my book. In fact, cold-calling is fun. I do like it now, because I am indeed helping others by offering my services. Thank you for the 'coaching' you provided me . . . You've blessed me! I wish you all the best in helping others to make more sales." Joyce Li, Speaker & Author, *Reimagine Your Retirement*

(About Therese's book *Don't KILL the Sale Before You Show Up!*) "I like it . . . you know what you're talking about – it is not just untested theory." Stanley Silver, Smalltalk and JavaScript Programmer and Author

"Therese is . . . a true, ethical and talented business professional . . . an asset to anyone who she works with or coaches in best business practices." Julie Maguire, President, HCMM Inc.

(Comment on *Don't KILL the Sale Before You Show Up!*) "The content is gold, diamonds, rubies, platinum. The points you make are spot-on and extremely valuable, and the tone of the writing and presentation is gripping, engrossing, and exciting. I would have expected nothing less from you. You know this stuff – you've learned it through long experience – and you're very effective at communicating it to others." Steve Lenius, Owner, Movable Type & Marketing, Advertising Consultant, Writer and Author

"Therese is the consummate sales coach. She listens well, determines what I need and zeroes in on that. No wasted time. Straight to the point. I am adapting my thinking about sales and it's starting to become fun!" Reesa Woolf, PhD, Author of *Executive Speaking in a Weekend*

"I am eternally grateful for the (sales) coaching that you gave me. I've used it significantly since we developed it and it's been very useful." Mark Hargis, Partner, Stohlmann Hargis Financial Group

"Wow, Therese Samudio is the marketer that thinks outside the box! Whether guiding a group of store managers to set sales goals or motivating them to perform, she is a top notch Sales Speaker and Coach. On a shoestring budget, she promoted our mall and led a group of 110 merchants to their best-ever performance (an 18% increase in annual sales when the other regional shopping malls in the area were in decline). Marketing the property out of the doldrums resulted in a million dollars in profit within a year and led to dramatically increased occupancy. I would always work on another project with her." Mark Norgaard, Real Estate Developer